First Facts™

Manners

Manners on the Telephone

by Terri DeGezelle

Consultant:
Madonna Murphy, PhD, Professor of Education
University of St. Francis, Joliet, Illinois
Author, *Character Education in America's Blue Ribbon Schools*

Capstone
press
Mankato, Minnesota

First Facts is published by Capstone Press
151 Good Counsel Drive, P.O. Box 669, Mankato, Minnesota 56002
www.capstonepress.com

Library of Congress Cataloging-in-Publication Data
DeGezelle, Terri, 1955–
     Manners on the telephone / by Terri DeGezelle.
     p. cm.—(First facts. Manners)
     Includes bibliographical references and index.
     ISBN 0-7368-2648-3 (hardcover)
     1. Telephone etiquette—Juvenile literature. [1. Telephone etiquette. 2. Etiquette.] I. Title.
II. Series.
BJ2195.D44 2005
395.5′9—dc22   2003023369

Summary: Explains good manners and shows how different manners and character values can
     be used when making and answering telephone calls. Includes information on telephone
     safety and calling emergency numbers.

Editorial Credits
Christine Peterson, editor; Juliette Peters, designer; Wanda Winch, photo researcher; Eric Kudalis,
     product planning editor

Photo Credits
Capstone Press/Gem Photo Studio/Dan Delaney, cover (foreground), 4–5, 7, 8, 9, 10–11, 12–13, 14,
     15, 16, 17, 18–19
Getty Images/Hulton Archive, 20
Photodisc Inc./PhotoLink/C. Borland, cover (background)

1 2 3 4 5 6 09 08 07 06 05 04

Table of Contents

Manners Are Helpful

Manners are helpful when using the telephone. People use good manners when they are polite and kind to others. Good telephone manners help people talk to friends, take **messages**, and call for help.

Showing Courtesy

People show **courtesy** when they use kind words. Kids can show courtesy when making a telephone call. When someone answers, Katie says, "Hello, may I speak to Wendy?" Katie says, "Thank you," and waits for her friend to answer.

Fun Fact!

In the United States, at least 140 million people use cell phones.

Being Polite

People can be polite when they answer the telephone. Polite people nicely say "hello." They listen to the caller without **interrupting**.

People can politely handle calls for others. They ask the caller to please wait. They hand the telephone to the person who has a call.

Being Responsible

People can be responsible when taking telephone messages. They ask for the callers' names and telephone numbers. They write the messages down on pieces of paper. They make sure people get their messages.

> **Fun Fact!**
> In 1929, Herbert Hoover became the first U.S. president to have a telephone at his desk.

People Cooperate

People can **cooperate** when others are waiting to use the telephone. People cooperate by taking turns. They can keep their conversations short. They let others use the telephone.

Fun Fact!
In the United States, 88 million homes have at least one telephone.

Following Rules

Parents often make rules about the telephone. Rules help keep kids safe. Rules let kids know what to say on the telephone.

Dispatchers ask many questions. They ask what happened. They ask if anyone is hurt. Dispatchers then know what kind of help to send.

Good Manners

Good manners are important when using the telephone. People can be polite when talking to others. They can be responsible when taking messages. They follow safety rules. Good manners help everyone enjoy using the telephone.

Amazing but True!

In the early 1900s, most telephone operators were women. These women were paid $7 a week to connect people's calls. Operators sometimes answered 600 calls in one hour. At that time, people also called operators to ask about weather and other news.

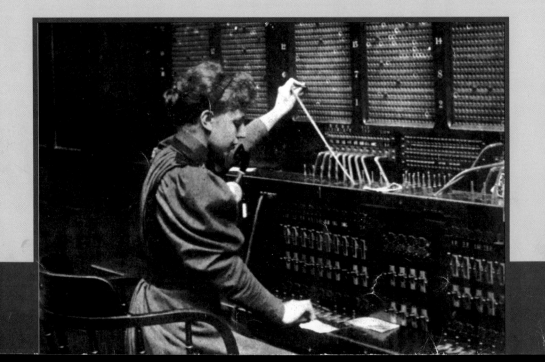

Hands On: Safety Card

Dispatchers help people who call 911 and other emergency numbers. Dispatchers ask questions and send help. Make a phone safety card so that important information is ready in case of an emergency.

What You Need

red marker
3-inch by 5-inch (8-centimeter by 13-centimeter) index card
pencil or pen
tape

What You Do

1. Using a red marker, write 911 across the top of the index card.
2. Print your name on the next line with a pencil or pen.
3. Write your address on the next line of the card.
4. Then write your home telephone number on the fourth line.
5. Tape the index card near a telephone in your house.

Glossary

cooperate (koh-OP-uh-rate)—to work with others and to follow rules

courtesy (KUR-tuh-see)—behaving in a way that shows good behavior toward others

dispatcher (diss-PACH-ur)—a person who answers 911 calls and sends rescue workers

emergency (e-MUR-juhn-see)—a sudden and dangerous situation that must be handled quickly

interrupt (in-tuh-RUHPT)—to start talking before someone else has finished speaking

manners (MAN-urss)—polite behavior

message (MESS-ij)—information that is given or sent to someone

Read More

Amos, Janine. *Hello.* Courteous Kids. Milwaukee: Gareth Stevens, 2001.

Mander, Lelia. *Answer the Phone.* Step Back Science Series. San Diego: Blackbirch Press, 2004.

Raatma, Lucia. *Politeness.* Character Education. Mankato, Minn.: Bridgestone Books, 2002.

Internet Sites

FactHound offers a safe, fun way to find Internet sites related to this book. All of the sites on FactHound have been researched by our staff.

Here's how:
1. Visit *www.facthound.com*
2. Type in this special code **0736826483** for age-appropriate sites. Or enter a search word related to this book for a more general search.
3. Click on **Fetch It** button.

FactHound will fetch the best sites for you!

Index